BESTIARY

or

The Parade of Orpheus

GUILLAUME APOLLINAIRE

BESTIARY

or The Parade of Orpheus

Woodcuts by Raoul Dufy

Translated by Pepe Karmel

DAVID R. GODINE, PUBLISHER · BOSTON

First published in 1980 by
David R. Godine, Publisher, Inc.
Post Office Box 450
Jaffrey, New Hampshire 03452
www.godine.com

Library of Congress Cataloging-in-Publication Data
[Bestiaire. English]
    Bestiary, or, The parade of Orpheus / Guillaume
    Apollinaire ; woodcuts by Raoul Dufy ; translated by
    Pepe Karmel.
        p.   cm.
      ISBN 1–56792–142–6 (softcover : alk. paper)
        I. Title: Bestiary. II. Title: Parade of Orpheus.
        III. Dufy, Raoul, 1877–1953. IV. Karmel, Pepe. V.
        Title
    PQ2601.P6 B413 2000
    841´.912—dc21   00–089373

Printed in the United States of America

Contents

Translator's Note

In translating you always have to give something up in order to save what you think is most important. The particular difficulty in translating Apollinaire's *Bestiary* lies in attempting to recreate Apollinaire's delicate balance between traditional, simple lyricism and modernist liberty. The poems are all very short, and not a few of them are rather slight in substance, so that much of their charm resides in the simple but pleasing rhymes and compact lines. In practical terms this meant there was a good argument for a rhymed translation.

Paradoxically, it was the brevity of the poems that dissuaded me from this course. Rhymed translations always compel a certain degree of distortion: the translator inevitably ends up leaving out things that were in the original and adding other words and conceits of his own invention in order to fill out the line and the rhyme. In a long poem, with luck, the translator can remain faithful to the overall narrative and tone even while taking some liberties on a line-by-line basis. In poems as short as those of *Bestiary*, however, every word and image counts, and even a small omission or addition is likely to alter drastically the effect of the poem. You might add or subtract a few brushstrokes from a vast canvas of a Tintoretto without noticing, but the slightest modification of a Cézanne watercolor would be instantly noticeable — and probably disastrous.

Obviously, no translation can avoid distorting the original, and the omission of rhyme here is a radical change in its own right. It seemed to me that the best way to remain as faithful as possible to Apollinaire's vision was not to strain after rhymes unless they came naturally, but to seek to maintain the tone of the lines. Apollinaire's voice in *Bestiary* varies from the colloquial to the solemnly impassioned, as befits a poet who, after a religious adolescence, supported himself by writing pornography. The poems of *Bestiary* mingle lyric imagery with a bawdy sense of humor, flashes of sincere religiosity, and the melodious rhythms of the folk song or nursery rhyme. In the notes he himself provided to the poems, Apollinaire cites an old lyric that seems to have inspired him:

> To shelter Rosemonde from the malice
> She suffered from his queen,
> The king built Rosemonde a palace
> More beautiful than ever seen.

But Apollinaire's modern reconstruction of Rosemonde's palace is a poem about bugs!

I would like to thank Megan Marshall, Sarah Saint-Onge, William B. Goodman, and Steven Cramer for their advice. Whatever felicities the reader may find in these translations should be credited to them; the faults are all my own.

— *Pepe Karmel*

Biographical Note

Guillaume Apollinaire was born in Rome on August 26, 1880. The son of a sometime adventuress, Angelica Kostrowitzky, and an unknown father, he was baptised Gugliemo Alberto Wladimiro Alessandro Apollinaro Kostrowitzky. His turbulent childhood was governed by his mother's passion for gambling. He first heard French in Monte Carlo. Rarely in one place long enough to finish a school year, young Kostrowitzky was nonetheless composing poetry long before he took the name of Apollinaire.

At age nineteen, Apollinaire moved to Paris and took a series of hack writing jobs. Broke, he drifted in and out of the city. In August 1901 he became tutor to the children of the Viscountess of Milhau. Their governess, Annie Playden, became the first great love of his life, inspiring some of his most famous poems.

In 1903, back in Paris after a stint abroad working for the Viscountess, Apollinaire met André Salmon, Alfred Jarry, and Jean Moréas. He made his debut in the Paris literary scene by founding *Le Festin d'Esope*, a periodical that went out of business in less than a year. Early in 1904 he met Max Jacob and Pablo Picasso, and in the spring of 1905 he began editing the *Revue Immoraliste*. This too failed, and by 1906 he was supporting himself by writing pornography.

Despite these setbacks, Apollinaire's importance in the art world grew rapidly. An influential champion of Cubism, the then revolutionary art style, he also coined the word 'Surrealism' seven years before André Breton formally founded the movement. His circle of friends included Braque, Picasso,

Dufy, 'Douanier' Rousseau, and Marie Laurencin (who became his mistress in 1907).

His first collections of poems, *The Rotting Enchanter*, was published in 1909; *The Heresiarch and Company* followed in 1910; and the next year, while working for the *Mercure de France*, his *Bestiary, or the Parade of Orpheus* appeared. These triumphs were overshadowed, however, when he was falsely arrested in connection with the theft of the *Mona Lisa* in September 1911; although he was released a mere five days later, the incident earned him considerable unsavory notoriety.

Marie Laurencin left him in 1912 and Apollinaire moved to the Latin Quarter. The following February he became the editor of *Les Soirées de Paris* and that same year he published *Alcools*, *The Cubist Painters*, and *The Futurist Antitradition*.

When war was declared in 1914, Apollinaire tried to enlist. At first unsuccessful, he finally managed to join the infantry in December, after an affair with the Countess Louise de Coligny (later immortalized in 'Lettres à Lou'). By the summer of 1915, he had been promoted to sergeant and become engaged to Madeleine Page, whom he had met during his service in Nîmes.

In November, Apollinaire joined the infantry as second lieutenant. On March 17, 1916 he received a serious head wound and was trepanned that May. Demobilized (but undaunted), he published *The Assassinated Poet* later that year. *The Breasts of Tieresias* followed in June 1917, and in November he gave his influential lecture on the 'esprit nouveau.'

In May 1918, Madeleine forgotten, he married Jacqueline Kolb, and his final collection of poetry, *Calligrammes*, was published. That November, two days before the Armistice, he died in Paris of the Spanish flu.

BESTIARY

or

The Parade of Orpheus

Orpheus

Admire the awful strength!
The noble lines:
His the speaking voice of light
As Hermes Trismegistus said in his Pimander.

Orphée

Admirez le pouvoir insigne
Et la noblesse de la ligne:
Elle est la voix que la lumière fit entendre
Et dont parle Hermès Trismégiste en son Pimandre.

2

The Tortoise

From magic Thrace, this madness!
My expert fingers ring across the lyre.
The animals move to my songs,
The sound my tortoise makes.

La tortue

Du Thrace magique, ô délire!
Mes doigts sûrs font sonner la lyre.
Les animaux passent aux sons
De ma tortue, de mes chansons.

The Horse

My formal dreams will harness you; my fate,
Riding a gold car, will be your handsome driver;
And, strained to frenzy, his reins will be
My lines, paragons of verse.

Le cheval

Mes durs rêves formels sauront te chevaucher,
Mon destin au char d'or sera ton beau cocher
Qui pour rênes tiendra tendus à frénésie,
Mes vers, les parangons de toute poésie.

The Tibetan Goat

For all this goat's fine wool,
Or even Jason's hardwon fleece,
I wouldn't trade a single hair
From the head of my beloved.

La chèvre du Tibet

Les poils de cette chèvre et même
Ceux d'or pour qui prit tant de peine
Jason, ne valent rien au prix
Des cheveux dont je suis épris.

The Serpent

You torment beauty.
How many women
Has your cruelty claimed!
Eurydice, Eve, Cleopatra;
And several others I could name.

Le serpent

Tu t'acharnes sur la beauté.
Et quelles femmes ont été
Victimes de ta cruauté!
Eve, Eurydice, Cléopâtre;
J'en connais encor trois ou quatre.

The Cat

In my house I want:
A reasonable woman,
A cat passing among the books,
And friends in every season,
Whom I cannot live without.

Le chat

Je souhaite dans ma maison:
Une femme ayant sa raison,
Un chat passant parmi les livres,
Des amis en toute saison
Sans lesquels je ne peux pas vivre.

The Lion

O lion, unhappy image
Of sadly fallen kings,
You are born now in a cage,
In Hamburg, among the Germans.

Le lion

O lion, malheureuse image
Des rois chus lamentablement,
Tu ne nais maintenant qu'en cage
A Hambourg, chez les Allemands.

The Hare

Avoid the lechery and fear
Of hare and lover,
But may your mind be always
Filled with child,
Like the hare's mate.

Le lièvre

Ne sois pas lascif et peureux
Comme le lièvre et l'amoureux.
Mais que toujours ton cerveau soit
La hase pleine qui conçoit.

The Rabbit

I know another coney
I'd like to take alive.
His warren lies among the thyme
In the tender land of love.

Le lapin

Je connais un autre connin
Que tout vivant je voudrais prendre.
Sa garenne est parmi le thym
Des vallons du pays de Tendre.

The Dromedary

With his four dromedaries
Don Pedro d'Alfarubeyra
Traveled the world and marveled.
He did what I would do,
If I had four dromedaries.

Le dromadaire

Avec ses quatre dromadaires
Don Pedro d'Alfaroubeira
Courut le monde et l'admira.
Il fit ce que je voudrais faire
Si j'avais quatre dromadaires.

The Mouse

Beautiful days, mice of time,
Bit by bit you gnaw my life away.
God! Soon I will have lived
Twenty-eight years, and badly.

La souris

Belles journées, souris du temps,
Vous rongez peu à peu ma vie.
Dieu! Je vais avoir vingt-huit ans,
Et mal vécus, à mon envie.

The Elephant

Like an elephant with his ivory,
I hold a treasure in my mouth.
Purple death! . . . I buy my fame
With sweetly singing words.

L'éléphant

Comme un éléphant son ivoire,
J'ai en bouche un bien précieux.
Pourpre mort! . . . J'achète ma gloire
Au prix des mots mélodieux.

Orpheus

Look at this lousy crowd,
A thousand feet, a hundred eyes:
Rotifers and insects, mites
And microbes – all more wonderful
Than the seven wonders of the world
Or even Rosemonde's palace!

Orphée

Regardez cette troupe infecte
Aux mille pattes, aux cent yeux:
Rotifères, cirons, insectes
Et microbes plus merveilleux
Que les sept merveilles du monde
Et le palais de Rosemonde!

The Caterpillar

Hard work leads to riches.
Poor poets, let us work!
The caterpillar, endlessly toiling,
Becomes the wealthy butterfly.

La chenille

Le travail mène à la richesse.
Pauvres poètes, travaillons!
La chenille en peinant sans cesse
Devient le riche papillon.

The Fly

Our flies know songs
They learned in Norway
From the enchanted flies
Who are the gods of snow.

La mouche

Nos mouches savent des chansons
Que leur apprirent en Norvège
Les mouches ganiques qui sont
Les divinités de la neige.

The Flea

Fleas, friends, even lovers,
How cruel are those who love us!
For them we bleed away our lives.
The well-loved are not happy.

La puce

Puces, amis, amantes même,
Qu'ils sont cruels ceux qui nous aiment!
Tout notre sang coule pour eux.
Les bien-aimés sont malheureux.

The Grasshopper

See the fine grasshopper,
That nourished Saint John.
May my verses be like him,
A feast for the best of men.

La sauterelle

Voici la fine sauterelle,
La nourriture de saint Jean.
Puissent mes vers être comme elle,
Le régal des meilleures gens.

Orpheus

Let your heart be the bait, the sky your pond!
Sinner, what salt water fish or fresh
Can match the beauty and the savor
Of that divine fish, JESUS, my Savior?

Orphée

Que ton coeur soit l'appât et le cièl, la piscine!
Car, pécheur, quel poisson d'eau douce ou bien marine
Egale-t-il, et par la forme et la saveur,
Ce beau poisson divin qu'est JESUS, Mon Sauveur?

The Dolphin

Dolphins, you play in the sea,
But the waves are always bitter.
Do I sometimes laugh with joy?
Life is still cruel.

Le dauphin

Dauphins, vous jouez dans la mer,
Mais le flot est toujours amer.
Parfois, ma joie éclate-t-elle?
La vie est encore cruelle.

The Octopus

Spraying his ink toward heaven,
Sucking the blood from those he loves,
And finding it delicious:
This inhuman monster is myself.

Le poulpe

Jetant son encre vers les cieux,
Suçant le sang de ce qu'il aime
Et le trouvant délicieux,
Ce monstre inhumain, c'est moi-même.

The Jellyfish

Medusas, gloomy heads
Of violet hair,
You delight in tempests,
And I too love them as you do.

La méduse

Méduses, malheureuses têtes
Aux chevelures violettes
Vous vous plaisez dans les tempêtes,
Et je m'y plais comme vous faites.

The Crayfish

Uncertainty,
O my joys,
Like crayfish we advance
Backwards, backwards.

L'écrevisse

Incertitude, ô mes délices
Vous et moi nous nous en allons
Comme s'en vont les écrevisses,
A reculons, à reculons.

The Carp

Carp, how long you live
In your crowded pools!
Fish of melancholy,
Does death forget you?

La carpe

Dans vos viviers, dans vos étangs,
Carpes, que vous vivez longtemps!
Est-ce que la mort vous oublie,
Poissons de la mélancolie.

Orpheus

The she-kingfisher,
Love, and winged Sirens
Know deadly songs,
Dangerous, inhuman songs.
Don't heed these wretched birds,
But hear the Angels of paradise.

Orphée

La femelle de l'alcyon,
L'Amour, les volantes Sirènes,
Savent de mortelles chansons
Dangereuses et inhumaines.
N'oyez pas ces oiseaux maudits,
Mais les Anges du paradis.

The Sirens

Sirens, do I understand your boredom,
Your laments resounding in the night?
I am like you, sea, full of subtle cries;
My singing ships are called the years.

Les sirènes

Saché-je d'où provient, Sirènes, votre ennui
Quand vous vous lamentez, au large, dans la nuit?
Mer, je suis comme toi, plein de voix machinées
Et mes vaisseaux chantants se nomment les années.

The Dove

Dove, the love and the spirit
That gave birth to Jesus,
Like you I love a Mary.
Please God that we may marry.

La colombe

Colombe, l'amour et l'esprit
Qui engendrâtes Jésus-Christ,
Comme vous j'aime une Marie.
Qu'avec elle je me marie.

The Peacock

When he spreads his tail, this bird
Who drags his plumage on the grass
May grow in beauty
But he also bares his ass.

Le paon

En faisant la roue, cet oiseau,
Dont le pennage traîne à terre,
Apparaît encore plus beau,
Mais se découvre le derrière.

The Owl

My poor heart is an owl,
Nailed, freed, and nailed again.
Its blood and strength are gone.
I praise all those who love me.

Le hibou

Mon pauvre coeur est un hibou
Qu'on cloue, qu'on décloue, qu'on recloue.
De sang, d'ardeur, il est à bout.
Tous ceux qui m'aiment, je les loue.

Ibis

Yes, I will go under the earth.
O certain death, let it be!
Fatal Latin, fearsome word,
Ibis, bird of the Nile banks.

Ibis

Oui, j'irai dans l'ombre terreuse
O mort certaine, ainsi soit-il!
Latin mortel, parole affreuse,
Ibis, oiseau des bords du Nil.

58

The Ox

This cherub praises paradise,
Where, near the angels,
We will live again, dear friends,
When the good Lord permits.

Le boeuf

Ce chérubin dit la louange
Du paradis, où, près des anges,
Nous revivrons, mes chers amis,
Quand le bon Dieu l'aura permis.

Notes

Admire the awful strength!
The noble lines

He praises the lines which form the pictures, magnificent ornaments of this poetic amusement.

His the speaking voice of light
As Hermes Trismegistus said in his Pimander.

We read in the 'Pimander': 'Soon the shadows descended ... and there came from them an inarticulate cry which seemed to be the voice of light.' This 'voice of light' is drawing itself, that is to say, line. And when light expresses itself completely, everything becomes colored. Painting is, properly, a language of light.

From magic Thrace

Orpheus came from Thrace. This sublime poet played a lyre given him by Mercury. it was made from a tortoise's shell, bound with leather, strung with sheep gut, with branches and a bridge. Mercury also gave lyres like this to Apollo and Amphion. When Orpheus played and sang, even savage animals came to hear his songs. Orpheus invented all the arts and sciences. Learned in magic, he could foresee the future and prophesied the coming of our Christian SAVIOR.

Filled with child,
Like the hare's mate.

The she-hare can conceive again while still pregnant.

> *With his four dromedaries*
> *Don Pedro d'Alfarubeyra*
> *Traveled the world and marveled.*

The famous account of his voyage, entitled 'Historia del Infante D. Pedro de Portugal, en la que se refiere lo que le sucedio en el viaje que hizo cuando anduvo las siete partes del mundo, compuesto por Gomez de Santistevan, uno de los doce que llevo en su compania el infante,' tells how the Infante of Portugal, don Pedro d'Alfarubeyra, set out with twelve companions to visit the seven parts of the world. These travelers rode four dromedaries and, after passing through Spain, went to Norway and, from there, to Babylon and the Holy Land. The Portuguese prince went on to visit the States of Prester John and returned to his own country after three years and four months.

> *Or even Rosemonde's palace!*

This palace was proof of the King of England's love for his mistress, as recounted in these lines from a 'complaint' whose author I do no know:

> To shelter Rosemonde from the malice
> She suffered from his queen,
> The king built Rosemonde a palace
> More beautiful than ever seen.

> *... the enchanted flies.*
> *Who are the gods of snow.*

Not all of them take the form of flakes, but many have been

tamed by the Finnish and Lapp wizards. The magicians hand them down from father to son and keep them shut up in boxes, ready to fly out in a swarm to torment thieves, while singing magic words which are as immortal as they.

See the fine grasshopper,
That nourished Saint John.

'Et erat Joannes vestitus pilis cameli, et zona pellicea, circa lumbos ejus, et locustas, et mel silvestre edebat.' Mark I:6

The she-king fisher,
Lover, and winged Sirens
Know deadly songs,
Dangerous, inhuman songs.

Sailors, hearing the song of the she-kingfisher, prepared to die, except in mid-December when these birds make their nests and the sea was believed to be calm. As for Love and the Sirens, these marvelous birds sing so harmoniously that life itself is not too high price to pay for the pleasure of hearing such music.

This cherub

Among the celestial hierarchies devoted to the service and glory of the divinity, there are beings of unknown forms and surprising beauty. The cherubim are winged oxen, not in the least monstrous.

When the good Lord permits.

Those who essay the art of poetry search for and love that perfection which is God Himself. Would this divine goodness, this supreme perfection abandon those who devote their lives to revealing His glory? It seems impossible. To my mind, poets have the right to hope that when they die they will attain the enduring happiness that comes with a complete knowledge of God, that is, of sublime beauty.

BESTIARY

has been composed by Michael & Winifred Bixler.
The typeface is Monotype Dante, designed by
Giovanni Mardersteig, cut in its original version by
Charles Malin, and first used in 1954. The mechan-
ical recutting by The Monotype Corporation of this
strong and elegant Renaissance design preserves
the liveliness, personality, and dignity of
the original.